# how2become

## Scottish Police Tests
## LANGUAGE

### www.How2Become.com

## by How2Become

Orders: Please contact How2Become Ltd, Suite 14, 50 Churchill Square Business Centre, Kings Hill, Kent ME19 4YU. You can also order via the e-mail address info@how2become.co.uk.

ISBN: 978-1910202272

First published in 2014 by How2Become Ltd

Copyright © 2016 How2Become.

Typeset for How2Become Ltd by Anton Pshinka.

Printed in Great Britain for How2Become Ltd by CMP (uk) Limited

Attend a 1 Day Police Officer Training
Course by visiting:

# www.PoliceCourse.co.uk

Get more products for passing Scottish
Police selection at:

# www.how2become.com

# CONTENTS

As part of this product you have received access to FREE online tests that will help you to pass the Scottish Police Tests!

To gain access, simply go to:

**www.PsychometricTestsOnline.co.uk**

## INTRODUCTION TO YOUR NEW GUIDE

Welcome to Scottish Police Language Tests: The ULTIMATE guide for helping you to pass the standard entrance test, for the Scottish Police service. This guide has been designed to help you prepare for, and pass the tough police officer selection process.

The selection process to join the police is highly competitive. Approximately 65,000 people apply to join the police every year. But what is even more staggering is that only approximately 7,000 of those applicants will be successful. You could view this as a worrying statistic, or alternatively you could view it that you are determined to be one of the 7,000 who are successful. Armed with this insider's guide, you have certainly taken the first step to passing the police officer selection process.

### About the Scottish Police Standard Entrance Test

The test is made up of three papers. There are three different versions of the test, therefore all applicants are allowed to sit the Standard Entrance Test (SET) a maximum of three times. The test covers:

- language
- numbers
- information handling

To help you get ready for the test, we've created sample LANGUAGE test questions for you to practice.

Work through each test carefully before checking your answers at the end of the test.

There are plenty of test questions for you to try out within this guide which are relevant to the LANGUAGE test element of the selection process. Once you have completed the testing booklet, you may wish to access our online police testing facility which you can find at:

# www.how2become.com

Don't ever give up on your dreams. If you really want to become a police officer, then you can do it. The way to approach the police officer selection process is to embark on a programme of 'in-depth' preparation and this guide will help you to do exactly that.

The police officer selection process is not easy to pass. Unless, that is, you put in plenty of preparation. Your preparation must be focused in the right areas, and also be comprehensive enough to give you every chance of success. This guide will teach you how to be a successful candidate.

The way to pass the police officer selection process is to develop your own skills and experiences around the core competencies that are required to become a police officer. Many candidates who apply to join the police will be unaware that the core competencies even exist. This guide has been specifically designed to help you prepare for the Police Initial Recruitment Test that forms part of the assessment centre.

If you need any further help with any element of the police officer selection process, including role play, written test and interview, then we offer a wide range of products to assist you. These are all available through our online shop www.how2become.com. We also run a 1-day intensive Police Officer Course. Details are available at the website:

# www.PoliceCourse.co.uk

Once again, thank you for your custom and we wish you every success in your pursuit to becoming a police officer.

*Work hard, stay focused and be what you want…*

**Best wishes,**

**The How2become Team**

# SECTION 1 –
# WARM UP EXERCISE 1

## WARM-UP QUESTIONS

Within the first section of this guide I have provided you with a number of sample warm-up questions that are based around the language test. This initial batch of 30 questions is different to the actual language test that forms part of the SET; however, they are great preparation for the real test and I would encourage you to try them. During the warm-up test you will be required to answer 30 questions in 10 minutes. This test is designed to assess and improve your English language skills. The test is multiple-choice in nature and in the real test you will have 4 or 5 options to choose from.

Take a look at the following sample question.

### Sample question 1

Which of the following words is the odd one out?

A. Spanner   B. Pliers   C. Hammer   D. Brush   E. Drill

The answer is D – brush. This is because all of the other items are tools and the brush is an item used for cleaning, and therefore is the odd one out.

Now take a look at the next sample question.

### Sample question 2

The following sentence has one word missing. Which word makes the best sense of the sentence?

*He had been ............ for hours and was starting to lose his concentration.*

A. studying   B. sleeping   C. complaining   D. walk   E. targeting

The correct answer is A – studying, as this word makes best sense of the sentence.

Now move onto warm-up exercise 1. There are 30 questions and you have 10 minutes in which to complete them.

## WARM-UP EXERCISE 1

### Question 1

Which of the following words is the odd one out?

A. Car   B. Aeroplane   C. Train   D. Bicycle   E. House

Answer [ E ]   ✓

### Question 2

Which of the following is the odd one out?

A. Right   B. White   C. Dart   D. Bright   E. Sight

Answer [ C ]   ✓

### Question 3

The following sentence has one word missing. Which word makes the best sense of the sentence?

*The mechanic worked on the car for 3 hours. At the end of the 3 hours he was _____ .*

A. home   B. rich   C. crying   D. exhausted   E. thinking

Answer [ D ]   ✓

### Question 4

The following sentence has two words missing. Which two words make the best sense of the sentence?

*The man _____ to walk along the beach with his dog. He threw the stick and the dog _____ it.*

A. hated/chose  B. decided/wanted  C. liked/chased  D. hurried/chased   E. hated/loved

Answer [ C ] ✓

## Question 5

In the line below, the word outside of the brackets will only go with three of the words inside the brackets to make longer words. Which one word will it NOT go with?

| A | B | C | D |
|---|---|---|---|
| In   (direct | famous | desirable | cart) |

Answer [ D ] ✓

## Question 6

In the line below, the word outside of the brackets will only go with three of the words inside the brackets to make longer words. Which one word will it NOT go with?

| A | B | C | D |
|---|---|---|---|
| In   (decisive | reference | destructible | convenience) |

Answer [ B ] ✓

## Question 7

In the line below, the word outside of the brackets will only go with three of the words inside the brackets to make longer words. Which one word will it NOT go with?

| A | B | C | D |
|---|---|---|---|
| A   (float | bout | part | peck) |

Answer [ D ] ✓

## Question 8

Which of the following words is the odd one out?

A. Pink    B. Green    C. Ball    D. Red    E. Grey

Answer [ C ]

## Question 9

Which of the following words is the odd one out?

A. Run    B. Jog    C. Walk    D. Sit    E. Sprint

Answer [ D ]

## Question 10

Which of the following words is the odd one out?

A. Eagle    B. Plane    C. Squirrel    D. Cloud    E. Bird

Answer [ D ]

## Question 11

Which of the following words is the odd one out?

A. Gold    B. Ivory    C. Platinum    D. Bronze    E. Silver

Answer [ B B ]

## Question 12

Which of the following words is the odd one out?

A. Pond    B. River    C. Stream    D. Brook    E. Ocean

Answer  | A |  ✓

## Question 13

Which of the following words is the odd one out?

A. Wood    B. Chair    C. Table    D. Cupboard    E. Stool

Answer  | A |  ✓

## Question 14

Which three letter word can be placed in front of the following words to make a new word?

Time    Break    Light    Dreamer

Answer  | DAY |  ✓

## Question 15

Which four letter word can be placed in front of the following words to make a new word?

Box    Bag    Age    Card

Answer  | POST |  ✓

## Question 16

The following sentence has one word missing. Which one word makes the best sense of the sentence?

*After walking for an hour in search of the dog, David decided it was time to turn ____D____ and go back home.*

A. up    B. in    C. home    D. around    E. through

Answer | D |

✓

## Question 17

The following sentence has one word missing. Which one word makes the best sense of the sentence?

*We are continually updating the site and would be _____ to hear any comments you may have.*

A. pleased    B. worried   C. available    D. suited   E. scared

Answer | A |

✓

## Question 18

The following sentence has two words missing. Which two words make the best sense of the sentence?

*The air force is made up of approximately 6,200 people, _____ is 11.5% of the _____ Royal Naval strength.*

A. which/total    B. and/total    C. which/predicted

D. and/corporate    E. which/approximately

Answer | A B |    x A

## Question 19

The following sentence has one word missing. Which one word makes the best sense of the sentence?

*The Navy has had to _____ and progress to be ever prepared to defend the British waters from rival forces.*

A. develop   B. manoeuvre   C. change   D. seek    E. watch

Answer | C |    x A

## Question 20

Which of the following words is the odd one out?

A. Cat    B. Dog    C. Hamster    D. Owl    E. Rabbit

Answer [ D ] ✓

## Question 21

Which word best fits the following sentence?

*My doctor says I _____ smoke. It's bad for my health.*

A. will    B. wouldn't    C. shouldn't    D. like    E. might

Answer [ C ] ✓

## Question 22

Which word best fits the following sentence?

*The best thing for a hangover is to go to bed and sleep it _____ .*

A. through    B. over    C. away    D. in    E. off

Answer [ E ] ✓

## Question 23

Complete the following sentence:

*By the time Jane arrived at the disco, Andrew _____ .*

A. hadn't gone   B. already left   C. has already left
D. had stayed    E. had already left

Answer [ E ] ✓

**Question 24**

Which of the following words is the odd one out?

A. Lawnmower  B. Hose  C. Rake  D. Carpet  E. Shovel

Answer [ ]

**Question 25**

Complete the following sentence:

*Karla was offered the job _____ having poor qualifications.*

A. although  B. even though  C. with  D. without  E. despite

Answer [ E ]

**Question 26**

Complete the following sentence:

*Not only _____ to Glasgow but he also visited many other places in Scotland too.*

A. did she   B. did he   C. did he go   D. she went

E. she saw

Answer [ C ]

**Question 27**

Complete the following sentence:

*Now please remember, you _____ the test until the teacher tells you to.*

A. shouldn't   B. will not be starting   C. are not to   D. can't  E. are not to start

Answer [ E ]

## Question 28

Which of the following is the odd one out?

A. Strawberry  B. Raspberry  C. Peach   D. Blackberry  E. Blueberry

Answer    | C |    ✓

## Question 29

Which of the following is the odd one out?

A. Football   B. Wrestling   C. Table tennis   D. Golf   E. Rugby

Answer    | B |    ✓

## Question 30

Which of the following is the odd one out?

A. Man    B. Milkman   C. Secretary   D. Police Officer  E.  Firefighter

Answer    | A |    ✓

Now that you have completed the warm-up exercise, check your answers carefully before moving on to the next batch of warm-up questions.

ANSWERS TO WARM-UP EXERCISE 1

27/30

1. E

2. C

3. D

4. C

5. D

6. B

7. D

8. C

9. D

10. C

11. B

12. A

13. A

14. Day

15. Post

16. D

17. A

18. A

19. A

20. D

21. C

22. E

23. E

24. D

25. E

26. C

27. E

28. C

29. B

30. A

## WARM-UP EXERCISE 2

### Question 1

I want to buy a new pair of jeans because I've put on _____ and my waist has expanded.

A. wait

B. weight

C. wheat

D. waite

Answer [ B ]

### Question 2

This week I felt so weak, I don't know why, maybe because I haven't _____ for days.

A. ate

B. eat

C. hate

D. eaten

Answer [ D ]

### Question 3

He'll go back to his country when there is _____ , but he might have to wait for years.

A. peice

B. peece

C. peese

D. peace

Answer [ D ] ✓

## Question 4

The new train was stationary for hours because of the _____ .

A. whether

B. weather

C. wether

D. weaver

Answer [ B ] ✓

## Question 5

_____ country is too dangerous so they're allowed to stay here.

A. Their

B. They're

C. There

D. Thare

Answer [ A ] ✓

## Question 6

I _____ some meat away because it tasted awful.

A. through

B. thru

C. threw

D. freed

Answer [ C ] ✓

## Question 7

He _____ his nose is big and people stare.

A. nose

B. knose

C. knows

D. nows

Answer [ C ]

## Question 8

_____ have to wait until tomorrow to get the results.

A. Heal

B. Hell

C. He'll

D. Heel

Answer [ C ]

## Question 9

Please do not worry, you are _____ alone.

A. not

B. knot

C. note

D. knote

Answer [ A ]

## Question 10

He decided to _____ for a while before carrying on with his journey.

A. paws

B. pores

C. pours

D. pause

Answer [ D ]

## Question 11

The teacher heaped _____ on the class for their hard work.

A. praise

B. preys

C. prise

D. prays

Answer [ A ]

## Question 12

Their mother said they were a right _____ when they got together.

A. pear

B. pair

C. pare

D. paer

Answer [ B ]

## Question 13

The police dog followed the _____ .

A. sent

B. cent

C. scent

D. scents

Answer [ C ]

## Question 14

The police decided to _____ the drugs.

A. seas

B. sees

C. seeze

D. seize

Answer [ D ]

## Question 15

Because the other team failed to turn up for the tournament, they got through on a _____ .

A. by

B. buy

C. bye

D. buye

Answer [ C ]

## ANSWERS TO WARM-UP EXERCISE 2

Q1. B

Q2. D

Q3. D

Q4. B

Q5. A

Q6. C

Q7. C

Q8. C

Q9. A

Q10. D

Q11. A

Q12. B

Q13. C

Q14. D

Q15. C

Now move onto the next section of the guide.

# SECTION 2 –
# JUMBLED UP SENTENCES

## JUMBLED UP SENTENCES

Within each question you will see a jumbled up sentence. Put the brackets containing parts of the sentence in the best order for the whole sentence to make sense. You are given the first two words of each sentence. Before you attempt the test, take a look at the following sample questions:

**Sample test question 1**

Carol expects (to make her) (me) (a party dress)

Answer: Carol expects me to make her a party dress.

**Sample test question 2**

What did (do) (out) (?) (with those) (had) (old) (thrown) (clothes I) (you)

Answer: What did you do with those old clothes I had thrown out?

Once you understand the test, move on to JUMBLED UP SENTENCES EXERCISE 1 which consist of 25 sample questions. You have 15 minutes to complete the test.

## JUMBLED UP SENTENCES EXERCISE 1

Within each question you will see a jumbled up sentence. Put the brackets containing parts of the sentence in the best order for the whole sentence to make sense. You are given the first two words of each sentence.

Q1. I drove to shops to (the) buy some fruit vegetables (and)

> I drove to the shops to buy some fruit + veg

Q2. It would (bitter fruit) (that) (foolish to) (eat) (be)

> It would be foolish to eat that bitter fruit

Q3. My mum (her) and (friend) wanted (go) to a (to) party (out)

My mom and her friend wanted to see out to a path

Q4. It would be (if she did not) a problem (do her homework)

It would be a problem if she did not do her hmwk

Q5. My brother (I) and went out (the) to park (a) on sunny day

My brother and I went out to the park on a sunny day

Q6. It would (important) be (her) moment in (an) academic career

It would be an important moment in her career

Q7. It would (a good idea) be (before going out to play) finish your homework (to)

It would be a good idea to finish your homework befor going to play.

Q8. James likes (at night) (his dog) (to walk)

James likes to walk his dog @ night

Q9. Reading sheet (is) music (tricky) (sometimes)

Reading sheet music is tricky somehtimes

Q10. Sarah is (to) keen (try) (team) (out) (for the)

Sarah is keen to try out for the team

Q11. Some dinosaurs (were) (than a) (two) (house) (taller) (storey)

Some dinosaurs were taller than a two storey house

Q12. John wanted (in the park) (to take the dog) (out for a walk)

John wanted to take the dog out for a walk in the park

Q13. Bella had (that she) (her work) (for) (was being assessed) (no idea)

Bella had no idea that she was being assessed for her work

Q14. James went (watch a) (to) (to Wembley Stadium) (football match)

James went to Wembley Station to watch a football match

Q15. The dog (chased the postman) (from the house) (and) (escaped)

The dog escaped + chased the postman from the house

Q16. The shopping (holiday) (for) (had closed) (centre) (bank)

The shopping centre had closed for bank holiday

Q17. Mia was (to) asked (the) (join) dance academy

Mia was ashed to jan the dance academy

Q18. My best (I) and friend (shopping) went for (mum's) my birthday

My best friend and I went shoppin for my mum's bday

Q19. I had to write 8,000 words (my) for dissertation. (was) it a relief (it was) when finished

I had to write 8,000 words for my dissertation It was a relief when it was finished

Q20. My mum (I) me (tells) sing (cannot)

My mum tell me I Cannot sing

Q21. I went (fishing) on a (trip) my with (brother)

I went on a fishing trip to my brother

Q22. I started (job) my (today) new. (was) I extremely nervous

I started my new job today. I was extremely nervous.

Q23. I like (read) to and (mystery) suspense books, (are) they exciting

I like to read mystery and suspence books they're exciting

Q24. I was (by) overwhelmed (thought) the

> I was overwhelmed by the thought

Q25. For lunch I (a) had a (sandwich) ham (cup) and of tea

> For lunch I had a ham sandwich and a cup
>
> of tea

Now check your answers on the following page.

25/25

## ANSWERS TO JUMBLED UP SENTENCES EXERCISE 1

1. I drove to the shops to buy some fruit and vegetables.

2. It would be foolish to eat that bitter fruit.

3. My mum and her friend wanted to go out to a party.

4. It would be a problem if she did not do her homework.

5. My brother and I went out to the park on a sunny day.

6. It would be an important moment in her academic career.

7. It would be a good idea to finish your homework before going out to play.

8. James likes to walk his dog at night.

9. Reading sheet music is sometimes tricky.

10. Sarah is keen to try out for the team.

11. Some dinosaurs were taller than a two storey house.

12. John wanted to take the dog out for a walk in the park.

13. Bella had no idea that she was being assessed for her work.

14. James went to Wembley Stadium to watch a football match.

15. The dog escaped from the house and chased the postman.

16. The shopping centre had closed for bank holiday.

17. Mia was asked to join the dance academy.

18. My best friend and I went shopping for my mum's birthday

19. I had to write 8,000 words for my dissertation. It was a relief when it was finished.

20. My mum tells me I cannot sing.

21. I went on a fishing trip with my brother.

22. I started my new job today. I was extremely nervous.

23. I like to read mystery and suspense books, they are exciting.

24. I was overwhelmed by the thought.

25. For lunch I had a ham sandwich and a cup of tea.

Once you have checked your answers please move onto exercise 2.

## JUMBLED UP SENTENCES EXERCISE 2

Within each question you will see a jumbled up sentence. Put the brackets containing parts of the sentence in the best order for the whole sentence to make sense. You are given the first two words of each sentence. You have 15 minutes to complete the test.

Q26. My boyfriend and (celebrated) (I) (one) our year anniversary

> My boyfriend and I Celebrated our one year anniversary

Q27. My favourite (is) film Saving Private Ryan because the (of) emotion and (line) story behind it

> My favourite film is Saving Private Ryan because of the ~~emotion and the~~ story line ~~be~~ and emotion behind it.

Q28. My happiest memory (a) is day of (snowy)

> My happiest memory is a day of snow

Q29. My best (party) birthday (when) was (I) 12. (went) we (was) ice skating (London) in

> My best birthday party was when I was 12. We went Ice skating in London

Q30. My favourite (of) type (is) dancing Latin and Ballroom

> My favourite type of dancing is Latin and Ballroom.

Q31. I like (watch) to the (leaves) the falling (the) in autumn

> I like to watch the leaves falling in the autumn

Q32. I like (drink) to (coffees) cappuccino and (biscuits) eat

> I like to eat drink cappuccino coffees and
> eat biscuits

Q33. It was (hot) a (sunny) and day, (I) so decided to (feed) and (go) the ducks

> It was a hot and sunny day, so I decided to
> go and feed the ducks

Q34. I received (not) detention for (attention) paying

> I recieved detention for not paying attention.

Q35. I like (go) to (in) singing (rain) the

> I like to so singing in the rain

Q36. Everyone is (on) going holiday (the) for summer

> Everyone is going on holiday for the summer

Q37. My mum (dad) and have decided (take) to us fishing

> My mum and dad have decided to take up fishing.

Q38. Camping is (a) way (great) to escape (some) for (and) peace quiet

> Campins is a great way to escape for some peace and quiet

Q39. All you (is) can do (best) your

> All yo can do is your best

Q40. The truth (absolute) is

> The truth is absolute.

Q41. A man's friend (best) (his) is dog

> A man's best friend is his dog

Q42. No one (left) (behind) gets or forgotten

> No one gets left behind or forsotten

Q43. Somebody told (this) me that is the (where) place everything (better) is and (safe) is everything

> Somebody told me that this is the place where everything is better and everything is safe

Q44. It is (things) funny how (out) turn

> It is funny how things turn out.

Q45. Life is (make) it what you

Life is what you make it.

Q46. On a (day) rainy, (sit) I indoors (have) and a duvet day

On a rainy day, I sit indoors and have a duvet day

Q47. I still (fairy) believe in tales

I still believe in fairy tales

Q48. Social media has (an) become (sensation) internet

Social media has become an internet sensation

Q49. Mr brother (I) and best (are) friends first, brother sister (and) second

My brother and I are best friends first, brother and sister second

Q50. On the weekends like (I) hanging out (my) with family and (films) watching

On the weekends I like hanging out with my family and watching films.

Now check your answers on the following page.

25/25

## ANSWERS TO JUMBLED UP SENTENCES EXERCISE 2

Q26. My boyfriend and I celebrated our one year anniversary.

Q27. My favourite film is Saving Private Ryan because of the emotion and story line behind it.

Q28. My happiest memory is of a snowy day.

Q29. My best birthday party was when I was 12. We went ice skating in London.

Q30. My favourite type of dancing is Latin and Ballroom.

Q31. I like to watch the leaves falling in the autumn.

Q32. I like to drink cappuccino coffees and eat biscuits.

Q33. It was a hot and sunny day, so I decided to go and feed the ducks.

Q34. I received detention for not paying attention.

Q35. I like to go singing in the rain.

Q36. Everyone is going on holiday for the summer.

Q37. My mum and dad have decided to take us fishing.

Q38. Camping is a great way to escape for some peace and quiet.

Q39. All you can do is your best.

Q40. The truth is absolute.

Q41. A man's best friend is his dog.

Q42. No one gets left behind or forgotten.

Q43. Somebody told me that this is the place where everything is better and everything is safe.

Q44. It is funny how things turn out.

Q45. Life is what you make it.

Q46. On a rainy day, I sit indoors and have a duvet day.

Q47. I still believe in fairy tales.

Q48. Social media has become an internet sensation.

Q49. My brother and I are best friends first, brother and sister second.

Q50. On the weekends I like hanging out with my family and watching films.

Once you have checked your answers please move onto exercise 3.

## JUMBLED UP SENTENCES EXERCISE 3

Within each question you will see a jumbled up sentence. Put the brackets containing parts of the sentence in the best order for the whole sentence to make sense. You are given the first two words of each sentence. You have 15 minutes to complete the test.

Q51. Sarah likes play (to) violin (the)

Q52. Sam likes (go) to training (the) at gym (times) five a week

Q53. My grandmother (I) and (her) walked dog one (evening) Sunday

Q54. Being a (officer) (police) is (very) a strenuous job

Q55. Nobody likes (left) to be behind

Q56. The aim (the) (for) class (to) was create (magazine) a cover

Q57. Sometimes Ryan like (feels) he (belong) doesn't

Q58. Nobody wants to (like) feel the ugly duckling (the) of family

Q59. It is important (your) for child to (the) know difference right (between) and wrong

Q60. If Sarah (her) does homework, (is) she (to) allowed watch an hour (television) of

Q61. My university course (a) is 3 year course (a) including year (placement) for

Q62. Winter is (favourite) James' (of) year (time)

Q63. Mia and (family) (her) always have (chicken) roast (a) on Sunday

Q64. In his (time) spare, (likes) Billy to go (skiing) water and wakeboarding

Q65. The police (always) are (the) outside nightclubs in town

Q66. Sarah's mum (a) bought (puppy) her for Christmas

Q67. It is to (difficult) drive (these) in foggy conditions

Q68. Harrison and family (his) went (all) down to (beach) the for a (weekend) long

Q69. Sam took (dog) his (a) for walk and (started) it to rain

Q70. I have a lot (worked) (I) this year, (think) I need a holiday

Q71. Sally went (to) (shopping) buy (dress) a new for a party

Q72. Two heads (than) (are) (one) better

Q73. Ryan's mum (him) grounded (for) having (party) a without (consent) her

Q74. The fireman (cat) saved (a) from (a) up tree

Q75. James likes (drink) to fizzy drinks but (dentist) (his) said (was) it bad (his) for teeth

Now check your answers on the following page.

# ANSWERS TO JUMBLED UP SENTENCES EXERCISE 3

Q51. Sarah likes to play the violin.

Q52. Sam likes to go training at the gym five times a week.

Q53. My grandmother and I walked her dog one Sunday evening.

Q54. Being a police officer is a very strenuous job.

Q55. Nobody likes to be left behind.

Q56. The aim for the class was to create a magazine cover.

Q57. Sometimes Ryan feels like he doesn't belong.

Q58. Nobody wants to feel like the ugly duckling of the family.

Q59. It is important for your child to know the difference between right and wrong.

Q60. If Sarah does her homework, she is allowed to watch an hour of television.

Q61. My university course is a 3 year course including a year for placement.

Q62. Winter is James' favourite time of year.

Q63. Mia and her family always have roast chicken on a Sunday.

Q64. In his spare time, Billy likes to go water skiing and wakeboarding.

Q65. The police are always outside the nightclubs in town.

Q66. Sarah's mum bought her a puppy for Christmas.

Q67. It is difficult to drive in these foggy conditions.

Q68. Harrison and his family all went down to the beach for a long weekend.

Q69. Sam took his dog for a walk and it started to rain.

Q70. I have worked a lot this year, I think I need a holiday.

Q71. Sally went shopping to buy a new dress for a party.

Q72. Two heads are better than one.

Q73. Ryan's mum grounded him for having a party without her consent.

Q74. The fireman saved a cat from up a tree.

Q75. James likes to drink fizzy drinks but his dentist said it was bad for his teeth.

Once you have checked your answers please move onto exercise 4.

## JUMBLED UP SENTENCES EXERCISE 4

Within each question you will see a jumbled up sentence. Put the brackets containing parts of the sentence in the best order for the whole sentence to make sense. You are given the first two words of each sentence. You have 15 minutes to complete the test.

Q76. Eve had appointment (an) (the) at doctors (she) because was not (well) feeling

Q77. Fred went (the) to opticians (he) because was getting (bad) really head-aches

Q78. The twins (climbing) enjoyed trees and (upside) hanging down

Q79. Sally's flower (is) shop (huge) a success (the) in summer

Q80. Liam and Millie (the) (went) to arcades to (air) play hockey

Q81. Tom went to (bank) (the) to draw (some) out money

Q82. Tom went (the) shops (to) buy (to) (sweets) some

<br><br><br>

Q83. My grandmother is (a) having party (celebrate) to her (birthday) 90th

<br><br><br>

Q84. Harry was (nervous) feeling (he) because had (test) a (the) in morning

<br><br><br>

Q85. When Sally (David) met, (had) she butterflies (her) in stomach

<br><br><br>

Q86. My grandmother and I (the) spent day in (garden) the planting flowers

<br><br><br>

Q87. Ryan is going (be) to left (alone) home because his (are) family going on holiday

<br><br><br>

Q88. Sam's nephew a (is) (genius;) computer (I) (turn) always to him (I) when have a technical problem

<br><br><br>

Q89. Miley had (audition) an (join) to rock (a) band

Q90. Harley had a (date) play with (best) his friend Chuck

Q91. Sam invited (friend) his to house (his) for dinner

Q92. Sue got (promotion) a (work) (at) and is celebrating (her) with family

Q93. Sam invited neighbour (his) round to (him) (help) (a) build shed

Q94. James loves (baseball) playing and (to) wants try out (the) for school team

Q95. A group (girls) of were out (the) in town celebrating (an) engagement

Q96. It was a (day) perfect to have (outdoors) an wedding

Q97. Peter and (friends) his (to) liked play video games

Q98. It was (sunny) a (and) warm day (be) to outside (Mia's) for graduation

Q99. Students were (nervously) waiting to (their) (get) exam results

Q100. Lucy went (for) out a (walk) at night and lost (got) (the) in woods

Now check your answers on the following page.

## ANSWERS TO JUMBLED UP SENTENCES EXERCISE 4

Q76. Eve had an appointment at the doctors because she was not feeling well.

Q77. Fred went to the opticians because he was getting really bad headaches.

Q78. The twins enjoyed climbing trees and hanging upside down.

Q79. Sally's flower shop is a huge success in the summer.

Q80. Liam and Millie went to the arcades to play air hockey.

Q81. Tom went to the bank to draw out some money.

Q82. Tom went to the shops to buy some sweets.

Q83. My grandmother is having a party to celebrate her 90th birthday.

Q84. Harry was feeling nervous because he had a test in the morning.

Q85. When Sally met David, she had butterflies in her stomach.

Q86. My grandmother and I spent the day in the garden planting flowers.

Q87. Ryan is going to be left home alone because his family are going on holiday.

Q88. Sam's nephew is a computer genius; I always turn to him when I have a technical problem.

Q89. Miley had an audition to join a rock band.

Q90. Harley had a play date with his best friend Chuck.

Q91. Sam invited his friend to his house for dinner.

Q92. Sue got a promotion at work and is celebrating with her family.

Q93. Sam invited his neighbour round to help him build a shed.

Q94. James loves playing baseball and wants to try out for the school team.

Q95. A group of girls were out in the town celebrating an engagement.

Q96. It was a perfect day to have an outdoors wedding.

Q97. Peter and his friends liked to play video games.

Q98. It was a sunny and warm day to be outside for Mia's graduation.

Q99. Students were waiting nervously to get their exam results.

Q100. Lucy went out for a walk at night and got lost in the woods.

Once you have checked your answers please move onto the next exercise.

# SECTION 3 –
# SENTENCES WITH
# MISSING WORDS

## SENTENCES WITH MISSING WORDS

This type of question requires you to fill in the missing blank in order for the sentence to read correctly. You have a choice of 4 words with which to fill the gap in each sentence. Select the word which best completes each sentence. Give one answer for each question. Study the examples below before you begin the four exercises to make sure you understand how to do the test.

### Sample question 1

Is this the place _____ you saw the accident?

1.which

2.when

3.where

4.who

Answer: where

### Sample question 2

The thief escaped _____ the open gate.

1.under

2.through

3.over

4.on

Answer: through

Once you understand the sample questions move onto the exercises that follow.

## SENTENCES WITH MISSING WORDS EXERCISE 1

There are 25 questions and you have 12 minutes to complete the test.

Q1. The same situation kept _____ .

1.occuring

2.ocurring

3.occurring

4.ocuring

Answer [ 3 ]    ✓

Q2. The finder was advised to take the umbrella to the lost _____ office.

1.propperty

2.proparty

3.property

4.properrty

Answer [ 3 property ]

Q3. Richard spent literally hours working on the same _____ of work.

1.peace

2.piece

3.piese

4.pees

Answer [ 2 piece ]

Q4. Sarah had to deal with an angry customer, but she did not deal with them _____ .

1.properlly

2.properly

3.properley

4.properrly

Answer | 2 properly |

Q5. She was asked to complete the job in the _____ manner.

1.usual

2.usule

3.usuall

4.yousual

Answer | Usual |

Q6. Sarah had no idea _____ she was going.

1.were

2.where

3.weir

4.wear

Answer | 2. where |

Q7. Sarah was the manager of a company and had to _____ all types of problems.

1.encounter

2.incounter

3.incountar

4.encountar

Answer [ *1 encounter* ]

Q8. Sarah went to the shops _____ she was hungry.
1. becaus
2. becauz
3. because
4. beecause

Answer [ *3 because* ]

Q9. Charlotte thought the room looked very _____ .
1. decodent
2. decadent
3. decodence
4. decadence

Answer [ *2 decadent* ]

Q10. Sarah thinks she may need to go and see an _____ .
1. opticion
2. optician
3. opticien
4. optishion

Answer [ *2 optician* ]

Q11. The teacher tried to give the students good _____ .
1. example
2. exemple

3.examples

4.exemples

*examples*

Answer | 4 3 |

Q12. For a musician you need to have _____ .

1.creative

2.cretivity

3.creativity

4.creativety

*creativity*

Answer | 3 |

Q13. In the factory, workers needed to use their _____ .

1.initiative

2.initative

3.enitiative

4.inishative

*initiative*

Answer | 1 |

Q14. The door to the cabin was left _____ .

1.unnlocked

2.unlocked

3.unllocked

4.unloked

*unlocked*

Answer | 2 |

Q15. The argument put forward by Rita had no _____ to the case.

1.significanse

2.significans

3.significance

4.significunce

Answer [ significance 3 ]

Q16. The _____ were extending the house.

1.builders

2.bilders

3.billders

4.buillders

Answer [ 1 ]

Q17. The students were asked to put forward a _____ towards the research.

1.propposition

2.proposition

3.proposishun

4.proposishan

Answer [ 2 ]

Q18. The glass lens in the _____ had smashed.

1.specticles

2.speticuls

3.specticals

4.spectacles

Answer | 4r

Q19. On a field trip, the students were asked to _____ the natural environment.

1.obsserv

2.observe

3.observation

4.obsurve

Answer | 2

Q20. The twins wanted to go for a walk but it was _____ wet.

1.two

2.too

3.to

4.tooh

Answer | 2

Q21. The doctors said that the man was in a critical but _____ condition.

1.staple

2.stable

3.stayble

4.staball

Answer | 2

Q22. Sending flowers to a funeral is a _____ gesture.

1.foughtful

2.thoughtful

3.faughtful

4.thortfall

Answer [ 2 ]

Q23. Geography students are taught how to look after the _____ .

1.invironment

2.envirament

3.environment

4.invirenment

Answer [ 3 ]

Q24. One of the students in the class always seemed to be a _____ .

1.probalem

2.problem

3.problam

4.probelem

Answer [ 2 ]

Q25. Steve and Michael _____ in a battle of thumb wars.

1.thought

2.fought

3.thwart

4.fault

Answer [ 2 ]

Now check your answers before moving on to the next exercise.

## ANSWERS TO SENTENCES WITH MISSING WORDS EXERCISE 1

1. occurring
2. property
3. piece
4. properly
5. usual
6. where
7. encounter
8. because
9. decadent
10. optician
11. examples
12. creativity
13. initiative
14. unlocked
15. significance
16. builders
17. proposition
18. spectacles
19. observe
20. too
21. stable
22. thoughtful
23. environment
24. problem
25. fought

Now move on to the next exercise.

## SENTENCES WITH MISSING WORDS EXERCISE 2

There are 25 questions and you have 12 minutes to complete the test.

Q26. The teacher told the child that his behaviour was not _____ .

1.exceptable

2.acceptable

3.acceptible

4.exceptible

Answer | *acceptable* |

Q27. The child was trying to _____ some knowledge for her class tomorrow.

1.equire

2.acquire

3.acwiar

4.acwire

Answer | *acquire* |

Q28. Sarah and Mia got in an _____ over the same boy.

1.argument

2.arguement

3.argumant

4.areguement

Answer | *argument* |

Q29. Sarah's birthday falls in the last _____ month.

1.calander

2.calendar

3.kalender

4.calindar

Answer [ *Calendar* ]

Q30. It was a _____ sunny day.

1.bewtiful

2.beutiful

3.beautiful

4.bueteful

Answer [ *beauhful* ]

Q31. The neighbour next door was a _____ man.

1.pompers

2.pompous

3.pomperse

4.pompouse

Answer [ *pompous* ]

Q32. Scientists discovered a new cure which is proving _____ .

1.fenomenal

2.phenomanall

3.phenomenal

4.fennomanal

Answer [ phenomenal. ]

Q33. My family have just got back from _____ .

1.Missisippi

2.Mississippi

3.Misisipi

4.Misissippi

Answer [ Mississippi ]

Q34. We went to a jumble sale and found some great _____ .

1.bargens

2.bargins

3.bargains

4.barggains

Answer [ ~~bargans~~ bargain ]

Q35. The work required _____ skills.

1.pacific

2.spacific

3.specific

4.spesific

Answer [ specific ]

Q36. The job looked promising but it was not _____ .

1.definate

2.deafinite

3.deffinite

4.definite

Answer  *definite*

Q37. Having a zero-hour contract does not _____ you any hours.

1.garante

2.garuntee

3.guarantee

4.guarantey

Answer  *guarantee*

Q38. The job needed someone to start _____ .

1.imideatley

2.emmediatley

3.immediately

4.immeadiatley

Answer  *immediately*

Q39. Please answer the questions using your _____ .

1.intelligence

2.intellegence

3.inteligence

4.intellegenc

Answer [ *intelligence* ]

Q40. Her favourite _____ activity was skiing.

1.leshure

2.lesuir

3.lesuire

4.leisure

Answer [ *lesohe* ]

Q41. You need a _____ to drive a car.

1.lisance

2.liceance

3.license

4.lisence

Answer [ *license* ]

Q42. John went to the _____ to research his paper.

1.liberary

2.library

3.librarey

4.lybrarey

Answer [ *library* ]

Q43. Sarah had a tricky _____ to do on her driving test.

1.manoovar

2.maneouver

3.maneuver

4.manoeuvre

Answer  | maneuvre |

Q44. We _____ go on holiday.

1.ocasionaly

2.occasionally

3.ocassionally

4.ocassionally

Answer  | occasionally occas |   occasionally

Q45. My teacher asked us to write a _____ .

1.playright

2.playwrite

3.playwright

4.playrite

Answer  | playwrite |   playwright

Q46. Holly's grandmother had some personal _____ .

1.poseshions

2.possession

3.possessions

4.posessions

Answer [ *possessions* ]

Q.47. Sarah knew that the snake was _____ .

1.poissonous

2.poisionous

3.poisonous

4.posinous

Answer [ *poisonous.* ]

Q48. Sarah's lips were_____ .

1.tremballing

2.trembling

3.trembaling

4.trembleing

Answer [ *trembling* ]

Q49. That book was a work of_____ .

1.ficshon

2.ficshion

3.fiction

4.ficttion

Answer [ *fiction* ]

Q50. That actress received a great deal of _____ .

1.publicity

2.publicaty

3.publisaty

4.publicate

Answer 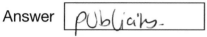 publicity.

Now check your answers before moving on to the next exercise.

## ANSWERS TO SENTENCES WITH MISSING WORDS EXERCISE 2

Q26. acceptable

Q27. acquire

Q28. argument

Q29. calendar

Q30. beautiful

Q31. pompous

Q32. phenomenal

Q33. Mississippi

Q34. bargains

Q35. specific

Q36. definite

Q37. guarantee

Q38. immediately

Q39. intelligence

Q40. leisure

Q41. license

Q42. library

Q43. manoeuvre

Q44. occasionally

Q45. playwright

Q46. possessions

Q.47. poisonous

Q48. trembling

Q49. fiction

Q50. publicity

Now move on to the next exercise.

## SENTENCES WITH MISSING WORDS EXERCISE 3

There are 25 questions and you have 12 minutes to complete the test.

Q51. Children need to learn the difference between wrong and _____ .

1.rite

2.write

3.right

4.writ

Answer | right |

Q52. The class had to fill out a _____ .

1.questionair

2.questionnaire

3.questionnair

4.cwestionare

Answer | queshonaire |

Q53. Ryan's friend _____ a war film.

1.recomend

2.reccomend

3.recommended

4.recamend

Answer | recommended |

Q54. Sarah needed a _____ for her college application.

1.refarance

2.referrense

3.reference

4.refference

Answer  [ reference ]

Q55. The class was asked to write a poem that _____ .

1.rimed

2.ryhmed

3.rhymed

4.rymed

Answer  [ rhymed ]

Q56. That teenager is _____ .

1.delinkwent

2.delinquant

3.delinquent

4.dellinquent

*delinquar*

Answer  [ delinquar ]  x *delinquent* ✓

Q57. Elizabeth was on a very strict _____ .

1.skedule

2.schedual

3.schedule

4.skedual

Answer  [ schedule ]

Q58. The_____ forecast is mostly cloudy.

1.whether

2.wearther

3.weaver

4.weather

Answer   weather

Q59. That document _____ a signature.

1.recwires

2.requires

3.requirres

4.recquires

Answer   requires

Q60. The scratch on the car was _____ .

1.noticeable

2.notiseable

3.notesable

4.noticeeble

Answer   noticeable

Q61.  Mark needed to work on his_____ .

1.pronunsiation

2.pronunciation

3.pronounciation

4.pronounsiasion

Answer [ pronunciation ]

Q62. Peter had a motorcycle _____ .

1.acxident

2.acident

3.accident

4.acciddent

Answer [ accident ]

Q63. Sarah's daughter _____ in fairy tales.

1.belleaves

2.beleives

3.believes

4.bellieves

Answer [ believes ]

Q64. Michael had to _____ a class of 30 pupils.

1.manige

2.manage

3.mannage

4.manege

Answer [ Manage ]

Q65. Tom played football at a _____ level.

1.professional

2.proffesional

3.proffessional

4.profeshonal

Answer [ *profesional* ]

Q66. The inn had to _____ for 30 guests.

1.acomodate

2.accomodate

3.accommodate

4.ackomodate

Answer [ *accomodate* ] ✗ *accommodate*

Q67. You should be _____ what you get at Christmas.

1.gratful

2.gratefull

3.grateful

4.greatfall

Answer [ *grateful* ]

Q68. The sports team did not have enough _____ for everyone.

1.equipmant

2.eqquipment

3.equipment

4.equippment

Answer *equipment*

Q69. That concert was _____ .

1.exilarateing

2.exhilarateing

3.exhilarating

4.exilerateing

Answer    exhilarahns

Q70. Sarah is good at _____ languages.

1.foran

2.foren

3.forengn

4.foreign

Answer    foreign

Q71. Mark's dream is not _____ .

1.imppossible

2.imposibble

3.impossible

4.emposible

Answer    impossible

Q72. Her new job made her feel _____ .

1.independant

2.indeependant

3.independent

4.indeppendent

Answer [ *independanr* ] ✗ *indenpendent*

Q73. Jack was being _____ .

1.insocial

2.unsocial

3.unsocail

4.insocail

Answer [ *unsocial* ]

Q74. Tom was being a _____ student.

1.dificult

2.difficult

3.difficalt

4.defficalt

Answer [ *difficult* ]

Q75. Fred liked to make a _____ entrance.

1.dramatick

2.dramateck

3.dramatic

4.drammatic

Answer [ *dramatic* ]

Now check your answers before moving on to the next exercise.

# ANSWERS TO SENTENCES WITH MISSING WORDS EXERCISE 3

Q51. right

Q52. questionnaire

Q53. recommended

Q54. reference

Q55. rhymed

Q56. delinquent

Q57. schedule

Q58. weather

Q59. requires

Q60. noticeable

Q61. pronunciation

Q62. accident

Q63. believes

Q64. manage

Q65. professional

Q66. accommodate

Q67. grateful

Q68. equipment

Q69. exhilarating

Q70. foreign

Q71. impossible

Q72. independent

Q73. unsocial

Q74. difficult

Q75. dramatic

Now move on to the next exercise.

**SENTENCES WITH MISSING WORDS EXERCISE 4**

There are 25 questions and you have 12 minutes to complete the test.

Q76. My family wanted to go on holiday to climb _____ .

1.mountins

2.mowntins

3.mountens

4.mountains

Answer | mountains

Q77. Hundreds of years ago, men and women had to follow the structure of_____ .

1.highrarkey

2.highrarcey

3.highrarcy

4.hierarchy

Answer | hierarchy

Q78. Tommy was being _____ .

1.ignorent

2.ignorant

3.iggnarant

4.ignarant

Answer | ignorant

Q79. His drawings were _____ .

1.emmaculate

2.immaculate

3.imaculat

4.immacullate

Answer    *immaculate*

Q80. _____ was building in the room.

1.tention

2.tension

3.tensesion

4.tenssion

Answer    *tension*

Q81. The application _____ was difficult.

1.proses

2.proces

3.process

4.proccess

Answer    *process*

Q82. Justin had great determination to _____ .

1.suceed

2.succed

3.succeed

4.suckseed

Answer | Succeed |

~~success~~

Q83. Martin had the _____ to carry on.

1.faultitude

2.fortitude

3.forrtetude

4.fortetude

Answer | forhhudi |

Q84. Lisa's mum told her _____ times to stop.

1.numberous

2.newmerous

3.numerous

4.numerrous

Answer | numerous |

Q85. His daughter was extremely _____ .

1.polight

2.powlite

3.pollite

4.polite

Answer | polite |

Q86. His recovery was _____ .

1.remarkeble

2.remarcable

3.remarkable

4.remarkabble

Answer  | *remarkable* |

Q87. His strength was _____ .

1.enspireing

2.inspireing

3.inspiring

4.enspiring

Answer  | *inspiring* |

Q88. Linda's boyfriend bought her _____ for her birthday.

1.jewlery

2.jewelery

3.jewellery

4.jewelry

Answer  | *jewellery* |

Q89. Tom has a _____ like a goldfish.

1.memary

2.memmery

3.memory

4.memmory

Answer  | *memory* |

Q90. Sam had to deliver an extremely important _____ to his boss.

1. dockyoument
2. doccument
3. document
4. doccumment

Answer     *document*

Q91. Rachel liked receiving _____ .

1. male
2. mail
3. mayal
4. maile

Answer     *mail*

Q92. Fliss enjoys to _____ .

1. read
2. red
3. reed
4. reade

Answer     *read*

Q93. Polly and her friends have a _____ to deliver in the morning.

1. precentation
2. presenttation
3. presentation
4. presentasion

Answer  | presentation |

Q94. Holly had to_____ her way round the woods.

1.navegate

2.navigat

3.navigate

4.navegate

Answer | navigate |

Q95. Andy was not good at putting together structured_____.

1.centenses

2.sentenses

3.sentences

4.sentances

Answer | sentences |

Q96. Tilly did not know the_____ to the last question in her exam.

1.anser

2.answar

3.answer

4.ancwer

Answer | answer |

Q97. Ryan did not know the sheer_____ of the event he was going to.

1.magnetude

2.magnitude

3.magnetud

4.magneetude

Answer    *masnitude*

Q98. John suffered major _____ to his head.

1.troremar

2.traumar

3.trauma

4.traurma

Answer    *traumar*

Q99. David's grandfather is a _____ man.

1.tradishional

2.tradichional

3.traditional

4.traditionnal

Answer    *tradihonal*

Q100. John's _____ is very new to the job.

1.college

2.colleage

3.colleague

4.coleague

Answer    *colleasue*

Now check your answers before moving on to the next exercise.

## ANSWERS TO SENTENCES WITH MISSING WORDS EXERCISE 4

Q76. mountains

Q77. hierarchy

Q78. ignorant

Q79. immaculate

Q80. tension

Q81. process

Q82. succeed

Q83. fortitude

Q84. numerous

Q85. polite

Q86. remarkable

Q87. inspiring

Q88. jewellery

Q89. memory

Q90. document

Q91. mail

Q92. read

Q93. presentation

Q94. navigate

Q95. sentences

Q96. answer

Q97. magnitude

Q98. trauma

Q99. traditional

Q100. colleague

Now move on to the next exercise.

# SECTION 4 –
# MISSING WORDS
# EXERCISE

## MISSING WORDS EXERCISE

### Question 1

You should read all of the passage below before you begin the test. You will see that there are missing words in the passage. Fill in each of the blanks by choosing the best word from the list below so that the passage makes sense. You have 5 minutes to complete the question.

> If you can't even arrive on ...*time*... for your interview, how is your employer supposed to ...*believe*... that you'll arrive on time for work? Plan to arrive for your interview with ...*plenty*. of time to spare, taking into account any traffic you may ...*encounter*... on the route. If you're not familiar with ...*where*... the job interview is taking ...*place*.. you might even want to locate it beforehand – ...*getting*... lost on the day will get you in a fluster before you've even had a chance to shake hands.

7 of the following 12 words have been taken out of the above passage.

Choose one word that best fits each blank space. Use your choice of word only once and write it down in the order in which you think it appears in the passage.

> time, believe, hands, chance, encounter, you, plan, where, place, plenty, account, getting

You may use this box to try out your ideas before filling in the blanks.

## Question 2

You should read all of the passage below before you begin the test. You will see that there are missing words in the passage. Fill in each of the blanks by choosing the best word from the list below so that the passage makes sense. You have 5 minutes to complete the question.

---

If you want to *appear* like you couldn't care less about getting the job or not then by all means avoid eye *contact* , slouch on your chair and occasionally crack your knuckles. This will give *your* interviewer the *impression* that you don't really want to be there and will help make sure you don't get the *job* . If on the other *hand* you want to show your *genuine* interest in the *position*, make sure you sit up straight, with your feet on the floor and *engage* your interviewer with appropriate levels of eye contact.

---

9 of the following 12 words have been taken out of the above passage.

Choose one word that best fits each blank space. Use your choice of word only once and write it down in the order in which you think it appears in the passage.

---

appear, contact, slouch, position, hand, feet, this, genuine, your, engage, impression, job

---

You may use this box to try out your ideas before filling in the blanks.

## Question 3

You should read all of the passage below before you begin the test. You will see that there are missing words in the passage. Fill in each of the blanks by choosing the best word from the list below so that the passage makes sense. You have 5 minutes to complete the question.

---

While an interviewer has ..reviewed.. your application and made their ..decision.. to grant you an interview based upon your qualification, how they interpret your ..appearance.. in the first few ..seconds.. of seeing you will most likely determine whether or not you get the ..position.. . They will pass judgement on whether you are the right ..person.. based on their reaction to how you walk, your handshake, how you ..sit...... and most importantly, how you are ..dressed.. .

---

8 of the following 12 words have been taken out of the above passage.

Choose one word that best fits each blank space. Use your choice of word only once and write it down in the order in which you think it appears in the passage.

---

decision, while, reviewed, appearance, seconds, person, dressed, position, seconds, based, sit, upon

---

You may use this box to try out your ideas before filling in the blanks.

## Question 4

You should read all of the passage below before you begin the test. You will see that there are missing words in the passage. Fill in each of the blanks by choosing the best word from the list below so that the passage makes sense. You have 5 minutes to complete the question.

Amidst talks of bringing private………. firms into ……….., the question simply begs to be asked: does it make ……….. to bring private ……….. into the police force, when members of staff are …………. but lack the …………. to be able to support officers fully? Would it perhaps make more sense if police ……….. were able to rely more on ……….., and would this require PCSOs to have more powers? These are questions that must be asked at a time like this.

8 of the following 12 words have been taken out of the above passage.

Choose one word that best fits each blank space. Use your choice of word only once and write it down in the order in which you think it appears in the passage.

buildings, policing, sense, devolution, available, powers, agencies, PCSO's, forces, security, politicians, craftsmanship

You may use this box to try out your ideas before filling in the blanks.

## Question 5

You should read all of the passage below before you begin the test. You will see that there are missing words in the passage. Fill in each of the blanks by choosing the best word from the list below so that the passage makes sense. You have 5 minutes to complete the question.

---

In recent times, as with most public services, the police force too has ........ unprecedented cuts. ........... of police officers and constables are ............ on the decline due to the severe ......... measures. At the same time, PCSOs whose role is to ............. the police force are ............. with few powers. At a time when the police force needs as much support from its entire staff as possible, should .............. be given more powers that would, arguably, make them more................ as the keepers of peace and ................ in the community?

---

9 of the following 14 words have been taken out of the above passage.

Choose one word that best fits each blank space. Use your choice of word only once and write it down in the order in which you think it appears in the passage.

---

faced, fresh, support, demonstrable, sharply, PCSO's, extrapolate, order, equipped, effective, austerity, diversity, numbers, beleaguered

---

You may use this box to try out your ideas before filling in the blanks.

## Question 6

You should read all of the passage below before you begin the test. You will see that there are missing words in the passage. Fill in each of the blanks by choosing the best word from the list below so that the passage makes sense. You have 5 minutes to complete the question.

All Emergency calls will be ……….. to the Fire department and it is this person that will answer calls initially. Good ……….. skills and …………., fast typing onto the Incident Format screen, are ………….. Once you become ……….. in this you will usually have an appliance ……….. to use before you finish your call. If the incident is likely to be of a larger nature or on a …………. for instance, then numerous calls will be received and everyone else, apart from the Radio position, will ……….. calls.

8 of the following 13 words have been taken out of the above passage.

Choose one word that best fits each blank space. Use your choice of word only once and write it down in the order in which you think it appears in the passage.

routed, in-depth, proficient, contagious, accurate, misrepresented, essential, motorway, answer, listening, en-route, failures, development

You may use this box to try out your ideas before filling in the blanks.

## Question 7

You should read all of the passage below before you begin the test. You will see that there are missing words in the passage. Fill in each of the blanks by choosing the best word from the list below so that the passage makes sense. You have 5 minutes to complete the question.

---

If you look at the ............. cause for those ............ , chances are you will find that it is confidence related brought about by a feeling of lack of ......... Someone goes into the assessment centre feeling ............. than prepared for a portion of the exam perhaps because they have tried to pass one of the tests before and ............. or perhaps because they know they have not studied enough. This is why ........... is essential especially in all matter of ways from ............. with another person, practical ............... with another person, and studying ............. written assessment questions.

---

9 of the following 14 words have been taken out of the above passage.

Choose one word that best fits each blank space. Use your choice of word only once and write it down in the order in which you think it appears in the passage.

---

root, disruptive, preparedness, multitude, less, assessment, tie, interviewing, practise, past, shoes, failed, nerves, conglomerate

---

You may use this box to try out your ideas before filling in the blanks.

## Question 8

You should read all of the passage below before you begin the test. You will see that there are missing words in the passage. Fill in each of the blanks by choosing the best word from the list below so that the passage makes sense. You have 5 minutes to complete the question.

By ............. your time to practise, ........... and know the assessment ........... you can walk into the assessment centre with your nerves under ............. You know you have prepared the best you could, ......... making costly errors in your preparation, and are ready to take on the assessment tests. Lastly, if necessary, find a place to ............., relax, and remember to be ............ and your ........... will remain in control.

8 of the following 13 words have been taken out of the above passage.

Choose one word that best fits each blank space. Use your choice of word only once and write it down in the order in which you think it appears in the passage.

measured, prioritising, criteria, mitigating, control, meditate, bolster, avoided, prepare, yourself, parliament, nerves, running

You may use this box to try out your ideas before filling in the blanks.

## Question 9

You should read all of the passage below before you begin the test. You will see that there are missing words in the passage. Fill in each of the blanks by choosing the best word from the list below so that the passage makes sense. You have 5 minutes to complete the question.

The best way to complete this is by ............. an event that has involved you within that ........... Write it as though the person you are ........... has no idea on the subject, and by reading it would under-stand the .............. you are explaining. I find that writing in a ............. context helps, as in a step-by-step direction. The more ............. you can put the better, although try not to ............ with useless ...........

8 of the following 12 words have been taken out of the above passage.

Choose one word that best fits each blank space. Use your choice of word only once and write it down in the order in which you think it appears in the passage.

describing, linger, informing, demystify, meeting, process, premedi-tated, content, information, 'waffle', 'diary', role

You may use this box to try out your ideas before filling in the blanks.

## Question 10

You should read all of the passage below before you begin the test. You will see that there are missing words in the passage. Fill in each of the blanks by choosing the best word from the list below so that the passage makes sense. You have 5 minutes to complete the question.

---

What is at the ……… of this affair is a shocking ………. of interest. The very same companies that seem to have ………... their wealthiest clients, mainly ……….. corporations and rich individuals to ………. tax, are those that have the …….….. to provide expert accountants to …………. the government on drafting tax laws and regulations. So the firms essentially helped their clients get away without paying tax by …………. loopholes from the same laws they helped to create.

---

8 of the following 12 words have been taken out of the above passage.

Choose one word that best fits each blank space. Use your choice of word only once and write it down in the order in which you think it appears in the passage.

---

Heart, heartless, aided, multiples, advise, power, avoid, distinguished, multinational, conflict, exploiting, rigour

---

You may use this box to try out your ideas before filling in the blanks.

# ANSWERS TO MISSING WORDS EXERCISE

## Question 1

If you can't even arrive on time for your interview, how is your employer supposed to believe that you'll arrive on time for work? Plan to arrive for your interview with plenty of time to spare, taking into account any traffic you may encounter on the route. If you're not familiar with where the job interview is taking place you might even want to locate it beforehand – getting lost on the day will get you in a fluster before you've even had a chance to shake hands.

- time
- believe
- plenty
- encounter
- where
- place
- getting

## Question 2

If you want to appear like you couldn't care less about getting the job or not then by all means avoid eye contact, slouch on your chair and occasionally crack your knuckles. This will give your interviewer the impression that you don't really want to be there and will help make sure you don't get the job. If on the other hand you want to show your genuine interest in the position, make sure you sit up straight, with your feet on the floor and engage your interviewer with appropriate levels of eye contact.

- appear
- contact
- your
- impression
- job
- hand
- genuine

- position
- engage

## Question 3

While an interviewer has reviewed your application and made their decision to grant you an interview based upon your qualification, how they interpret your appearance in the first few seconds of seeing you will most likely determine whether or not you get the position. They will pass judgement on whether you are the right person based on their reaction to how you walk, your handshake, how you sit and most importantly, how you are dressed.

- reviewed
- decision
- appearance
- seconds
- position
- person
- sit
- dressed

## Question 4

Amidst talks of bringing private security firms into policing, the question simply begs to be asked: does it make sense to bring private agencies into the police force, when members of staff are available but lack the powers to be able to support officers fully? Would it perhaps make more sense if police forces were able to rely more on PCSOs, and would this require PCSOs to have more powers? These are questions that must be asked at a time like this.

- security
- policing
- sense
- agencies
- available
- powers
- forces
- PCSO's

## Question 5

In recent times, as with most public services, the police force too has faced unprecedented cuts. Numbers of police officers and constables are sharply on the decline due to the severe austerity measures. At the same time, PC-SOs whose role is to support the police force are equipped with few powers. At a time when the police force needs as much support from its entire staff as possible, should PCSOs be given more powers that would, arguably, make them more effective as the keepers of peace and order in the community?

- faced
- numbers
- sharply
- austerity
- support
- equipped
- PCSO's
- effective
- order

## Question 6

All Emergency calls will be routed to the Fire department and it is this person that will answer calls initially. Good listening skills and accurate, fast typing onto the Incident Format screen, are essential. Once you become proficient in this you will usually have an appliance en-route to use before you finish your call. If the incident is likely to be of a larger nature or on a motorway for instance, then numerous calls will be received and everyone else, apart from the Radio position, will answer calls.

- routed
- listening
- accurate
- essential
- proficient
- en-route
- motorway
- answer

## Question 7

If you look at the root cause for those nerves, chances are you will find that it is confidence related brought about by a feeling of lack of preparedness. Someone goes into the assessment centre feeling less than prepared for a portion of the exam perhaps because they have tried to pass one of the tests before and failed or perhaps because they know they have not studied enough. This is why practise is essential especially in all matter of ways from interviewing with another person, practical assessment with another person, and studying past written assessment questions.

- root
- nerves
- preparedness
- Less
- failed
- practise
- interviewing
- assessment
- past

## Question 8

By prioritising your time to practise, prepare, and know the assessment criteria you can walk into the assessment centre with your nerves under control. You know you have prepared the best you could, avoided making costly errors in your preparation, and are ready to take on the assessment tests. Lastly, if necessary, find a place to meditate, relax, and remember to be yourself and your nerves will remain in control.

- prioritising
- prepare
- criteria
- control
- avoided
- meditate
- yourself
- nerves

## Question 9

The best way to complete this is by describing an event that has involved you within that role. Write it as though the person you are informing has no idea on the subject, and by reading it would understand the process you are explaining. I find that writing in a 'diary' context helps, as in a step-by-step direction. The more content you can put the better, although try not to 'waffle' with useless information.

- describing
- role
- informing
- process
- 'diary'
- content
- 'waffle'
- Information

## Question 10

What is at the heart of this affair is a shocking conflict of interest. The very same companies that seem to have aided their wealthiest clients, mainly multinational corporations and rich individuals to avoid tax, are those that have the power to provide expert accountants to advise the government on drafting tax laws and regulations. So the firms essentially helped their clients get away without paying tax by exploiting loopholes from the same laws they helped to create.

- heart
- conflict
- aided
- multinational
- avoid
- power
- advise
- exploiting

Now move on to the next exercise.

# SECTION 5 –
# ANALYSING INFORMATION
# EXERCISE

## Question 1

**Read the passage carefully. Answer the following 10 questions. Refer to the passage to find the answers. You have 10 minutes to complete the question.**

The time was 1600 hours when I was the teacher on patrol of the school gates of Waterloo infants. A distressed parent came running up to me shouting and crying. She stated that her 5 year old daughter Ana was supposed to meet her by the school gates at the end of the school day. Ana has sandy blonde hair and blue eyes and was wearing burgundy school uniform. The child had not been seen by anyone on the school premises for the past 45 minutes.

The primary school of Waterloo infants is based in a remote area of Hollingbourne that is surrounded by the countryside. Waterloo infants school is situated on the east side of the road. The front school yard sits on the main countryside road running in a north to south direction. This remote location is home to a post office, a pub and a local grocery store. Nothing for several miles is close. The nearest town is approximately half an hour away. As the police started to arrive to question the mother of the missing girl, it became clear that as time was going by, the whereabouts of missing 5 year old Ana seemed more daunting.

Nobody had seen Ana leave the school premises and her mother was confident that she would not just walk off by herself. The only lead the police had to go on was from a grandmother who was collecting her grandson from school. She told the police that about 1445 hours, she saw a strange man acting suspiciously outside Waterloo infants gates, and as she approached the school to collect her grandson, he scarpered off. This was the only lead the police had to go on, and so they set out a search party in order to find Ana. Door to door investigations were done, face to face inquiries were made. At approximately 1800 hours, after the police had spoken to many of the neighbours nearby, one of the neighbours came forward and made a statement. A woman said that she saw an identical man as to the one previously described. She told the police that around 1730 hours, she saw a man swiftly walking with a child – a child that fitted the same description of the missing girl.

As the search drew to a close, the police stumbled across some vital evidence. A hairband matching the description given by her mother and a burgundy jumper was found amongst some bushes on the outskirts of the countryside heading towards town. The police knew that they only had a matter of hours before it would begin to get dark and so they sent off for DNA samples of the evidence and waited for the results.

## Questions

1. Where was the patrolling teacher when she heard the news of missing Ana? *Waterloo infants*

2. Give a description of Ana. *Sandy blonde hair, age 5 blue eyes, burgundy school uniform*

3. Where is Waterloo Road situated? *East side, remote area > Hollinsbourne, surrounded by countryside*

4. How far away is the nearest town? *approximately half an hour away*

5. What is the one thing Ana's mother was adamant about to the police? *Ana would not walk up on her own*

6. What was the first lead the police had to go by? *A grandmother collecting her grandson, saw a man @ 1445 outside gate*

7. What time was it when the police received new information regarding missing Ana? *approximately 1800 hours*

8. What and who was the second statement given by regarding the case of Ana? *A woman said she saw an identical man as the one previously described. At 1730 she saw a man walking &*

9. What were the two pieces of vital evidence the police discovered? *child A hairband and burgundy jumper*

10. What were the police awaiting on as the search came to a standstill because of the darkness? *DNA samples of the evidence*

## Answers

1. Waterloo infants – school grounds.

2. Ana (aged 5) has sandy blonde hair and blue eyes and was wearing burgundy school uniform.

3. Based in a remote area of Hollingbourne that is surrounded by the country-side. Waterloo infants school is situated on the east side of the road.

4. Half an hour away.

5. That Ana would not walk off by herself.

6. A grandmother who was collecting her grandson from school. She told the police that about 1445 hours, she saw a strange man acting suspiciously outside Waterloo infants gates, and as she approached the school to collect her grandson, he scarpered off.

7. At approximately 1800 hours.

8. A woman said that she saw an identical man as to the one previously described. She told the police that around 1730 hours, she saw a man swiftly walking with a child.

9. A hairband matching the description given by her mother and a burgundy jumper was found amongst some bushes.

10. DNA samples of the evidence of the hairband and jumper.

## Question 2

**Read the passage carefully. Answer the following 10 questions. Refer to the passage to find the answers. You have 10 minutes to complete the question.**

At approximately 2130 hours, a woman phoned the police station. This woman, whose name remains anonymous, states that she just witnessed two young boys coming out of her local pub 'The Swan' on Aylesbury Road, Northampton, and then got into a black Mercedes car. She described the two young boys as being 18-19 and highly intoxicated.

The police followed through on this statement and dispatched a patrol car to go out and analyse the scenario. From the station to Aylesbury Road was a good 20 minute journey, so the police had to act quickly. They feared that the two boys who were described as "highly intoxicated" would cause an accident to themselves and/or others.

The woman stood by and waited for the police to arrive. At 2155 hours, the woman gave the police the number plate of the car and a description of both boys. One was tall, approximately 6ft, sandy blonde hair, with a mole of the left side of his face. He was wearing a blue chequered shirt, jeans and black loafers. The other boy was described as being roughly 5ft tall, dark brown hair and muscular built. He was wearing a black Fred Perry polo shirt with jeans and white Nike trainers.

Amidst the police taking a statement from this woman, they radioed the control centre the number plate of the car and asked for another patrol car to search the neighbourhood.

Meanwhile, at approximately 2225 hours, the police were called again. This time, it was from a man (Paul, 45) who was driving home from work who had witnessed a crash. The crash was 5 miles north of the area in which the boys had supposedly got into a car and drove intoxicated. When the police arrived at the scene, a black Mercedes was on its side. The car had evidently crashed into the tree and then flipped onto its side.

As the police waited for the paramedics to finish their job, they went over to investigate. However, only one person was in the car. It was the sandy blonde hair young boy that was wearing a chequered blue shirt. The police breathalysed the teenager and he was found to be over the limit. The police arrested the young boy but they had no idea as to the whereabouts of the other boy.

The police got back to the station at 2330 hours and put the boy in a cell for the night in order to sleep off the alcohol. He would be questioned in the morning.

## Questions

1. At what time was the police first called about an incident happening in Aylesbury Road?

2. What was the name of the woman who gave a statement about two drunk drivers?

3. The police received the call. It takes approximately 20 minutes to get to the described location. At what time would the police arrive at Aylesbury Road?

4. How did the woman describe the boy's state of mind when she saw them leaving the pub?

5. Give a description of both boys.

6. What happened at approximately at 2225 hours?

7. Where did the crash take place?

8. Which boy was the only one in the car?

9. What time did the police get back to the station with the young boy?

10. When would the boy be questioned and why?

## Answers

1. 2130 hours.

2. Anonymous.

3. 2150 hours.

4. Highly intoxicated.

5. One was a tall, about 6ft, sandy blonde hair with a mole of the left side of his face. He was wearing a blue chequered shirt, jeans and black loafers. The other boy was described as being roughly 5ft tall, dark brown hair and muscular built. He was wearing a black Fred Perry polo shirt with jeans and white Nike trainers.

6. A man phoned the police and told them about a crash he had just witnessed.

7. The crash was 5 miles north of the area in which the boys had supposedly got into a car and drove intoxicated.

8. The sandy blonde haired young boy that was wearing a chequered blue shirt.

9. 2330 hours.

10. In the morning, so it gave him time to sober up.

## Question 3

Read the passage carefully. Answer the following 10 questions. Refer to the passage to find the answers. You have 10 minutes to complete the question.

At approximately 2230 hours, PC Parker was on duty patrol in his local neighbourhood. The small village of Harlow was a place where everyone knew their neighbours. It was a small countryside village that was on the outskirts of the town Lincoln. The village was a horseshoe shaped village; it had a large green in the centre with a children's play park. To the left of the village contained a couple of small grocery stores, a pub and a doctor's surgery. To the right of the village was the local primary and secondary school. Houses were spread out around the edge so everything was at a glimpse of an eye.

Meanwhile, as PC Parker roamed the streets of Harlow, his radio went off. The message was that No. 8 High Street in Harlow had been broken into and needed someone to respond ASAP. PC Parker responded to the message and said he was already in that particular location. Due to the fact it was 2230 hours, it was dark and there were not many street lights lit in the area, so it was difficult to spot anything peculiar. PC Parker did not hear anything or see anyone acting suspiciously when he arrived at the scene of the alleged crime. As he entered No. 8, he met the owner of the house in the hallway. Mr Elliott Friend was the owner of the local shops nearby, he was 84 years old and was in total shock.

PC Parker took a look around the house to gather any evidence. He started from the back of the house and worked his way round to the front. He started in the kitchen that looked onto a courtyard with a built-in gate that led to a wooded area. As he circulated the kitchen, he noticed something peculiar. The window ledge had marks of dirt and dust. This seemed rather odd in what was a pristine looking kitchen where everything was in immaculate condition. As he investigated further, he noticed the lock on the window was missing and the window remained half open.

When PC Parker returned to the living room to talk to Mr Friend, he confirmed his suspicions. "I never leave the windows or doors unlocked", said Mr Friend. "I like this neighbourhood and I know every-one who lives here. It's my home and I can't believe someone would do this".

As PC Parker took another look around, he came across a ransacked room upstairs at the back of the house. This room was Mr Friend's bed-room. On examining the room further, he noticed a safe box on the floor. It had been broken into.

It was clear that this was an intended burglary which is believed to be worth thousands of pounds, including a limited edition golden watch that was stolen. The only thing that remained in the safe box was a picture of his beloved wife.

## Questions

1. Give a description of Harlow.

2. What message did PC Parker receive on his radio?

3. At what time was it when he received this message?

4. What no. was the house that had been broken into?

5. Who did the house belong to?

6. What was the first piece of evidence PC Parker noticed?

7. What did Mr Friend say to PC Parker regarding his home?

8. What room was ransacked?

9. What did PC Parker notice on the floor?

10. What was missing from the safe box and what was the only thing left?

## Answers

1. It was a small countryside village that was on the outskirts of the town Lincoln. The village was a horseshoe shaped village; it had a large green in the centre with a children's play park. To the left of the village contained a couple of small grocery stores, a pub and a doctor's surgery. To the right of the village was the local primary and secondary school.

2. The message was that No. 8 in Harlow had been broken into and needed someone to respond.

3. 2230 hours.

4. No.8.

5. Mr Elliott Friend was the owner of the local shops nearby, he was 84 years old.

6. The window ledge had marks of dirt and dust. This seemed rather odd in what was a pristine looking kitchen where everything was in immaculate condition. As he investigated further, he noticed the lock on the window was missing and the window remained half open.

7. "I never leave the windows or doors unlocked", said Mr Friend. "I like this neighbourhood and I know everyone who lives here. It's my home and I can't believe someone would do this".

8. Mr Friend's bedroom.

9. A safe box that was opened.

10. Thousands of pounds and a gold watch. The only thing that remained in the safe box was a picture of his beloved wife.

## Question 4

**Read the passage carefully. Answer the following 10 questions. Refer to the passage to find the answers. You have 10 minutes to complete the question.**

An ongoing investigation was taking place into the murder of a local girl. The girl was from the village of Madgingford. She was 20 years old and called Zoey Metcalfe. She had short blonde hair, blue eyes, petite figure and a girl everyone described as "sweet, caring and beautiful".

Her family and friends have all been questioned regarding her murder. Fingerprints and DNA were taken in order to rule people out and speed up the process of tracking down her killer.

Zoey Metcalfe was murdered on the 13th of February. Her body was found in a secluded wooded area approximately half a mile out from the village of Madgingford. The body was spotted at 1800 hours by a girl who was 8 years old. The 8 year old girl was in the wooded area with her mum and dad and their Border Collie, Alfie. When Alfie, darted in the opposite direction, the young girl instantly followed. About 5 minutes along a beaten old path across a lake, the young girl was seen by her parents with her border collie looking over the body of Zoey.

The police did not have much evidence to go on. They had sent off Zoey's clothes for forensic testing and had spoken to many people within the local neighbourhood.

The only piece of evidence they had to go on was an email sent to her the day before she was killed. At approximately 1545 hours, an email was sent to her asking to meet her in a café, just on the outskirts of the wooded area. The police tried to track who the message was sent from, but it was proving difficult. The message was sent from an email that no longer existed and was supposedly fake. The name in the email address does not exist in police files and the sender had disguised their IP address.

As the investigation remains ongoing, her family claimed that "Zoey is not the type of girl that would just walk alone at night in a wooded area."

As the days went by, her family were becoming agitated at the lack of progress. Her father was taking matters into his own hands and was questioning everyone he knew Zoey had a relationship with.

A couple of weeks later, Zoey's father was caught by the police shouting and grabbing a man that was supposedly dating his daughter. "You did it! I know you did it!" shouted Zoey's father. The man that was being grabbed, Gary, was allegedly dating his daughter, but he told her father that they broke up weeks before her death but that they still remained good friends. Her father was having none of it.

"Mr Metcalfe, if you don't calm down and stay out of the way, you'll slow down the progress even more. I know you want to know who killed Zoey, but you have to let the police do their job" (Police Family Liaison Officer, Sandra)

6 weeks later, the investigation into the death of Zoey Metcalfe remains ongoing.

## Questions

1. Give a description of the local girl who was murdered.

2. What was taken from her family and friends to speed up the process?

3. Where was Zoey's body found?

4. Give a description of how Zoey's body was found.

5. What did the police send away of Zoey's for testing?

6. What was the only piece of evidence the Police had to go on at the start of the investigation?

7. Why was this evidence proving difficult to follow?

8. Who took matters into their own hands?

9. What was Zoey's father caught doing by the police?

10. Why did Zoey's father believe Gary had something to do with the murder of his daughter?

**Answers**

1. The girl was from the village of Madgingford. She was 20 years old and called Zoey Metcalfe. She had short blonde hair, blue eyes, petite figure and a girl everyone described as "sweet, caring and beautiful".

2. Fingerprints and DNA were taken to rule people out and to speed up the process of tracking down her killer.

3. Her body was found in a secluded wooded area about half a mile out of the village of Madgingford.

4. The body was spotted at 1800 hours by a girl who was 8 years old. The 8 year old girl was in the wooded area with her mum and dad and their Border Collie, Alfie. When Alfie darted in the opposite direction, the young girl instantly followed. About 5 minutes along a beaten old path across a lake, the young girl was seen by her parents with her Border Collie looking over the body of Zoey.

5. Zoey's clothes.

6. An email was sent to her asking to meet her in a café, just on the outskirts of the wooded area.

7. The message was sent from an email that no longer existed and was supposedly fake. The name in the email address does not exist in police files and the sender had disguised their IP address.

8. Zoey's father.

9. Zoey's father was caught by the police shouting and grabbing a man that was supposedly dating his daughter. "You did it! I know you did it!"

10. Gary was allegedly dating his daughter, but he told her father that they broke up weeks before her death but that they still remained good friends.

Now move on to the next set of analysing information questions which take on a slightly different format. These questions are perfect for preparing for the SET language test. Answer the questions either TRUE, FALSE or IMPOSSIBLE TO SAY based ONLY on the information provided.

**Analysing information question 5**

You have 5 minutes to complete the question.

> **An accident occurred on the M6 motorway between junctions 8 and 9 southbound at 3pm. The driver of a Ford Fiesta was seen to pull into the middle lane without indicating, forcing another car to veer into the central reservation. One person suffered a broken arm and was taken to hospital before the police arrived.**

A = TRUE B = FALSE C = IMPOSSIBLE TO SAY

1. The accident was on the M6 motorway on the carriageway that leads to Scotland.

2. The driver of the Ford Fiesta was injured in the crash.

3. The central reservation was responsible for the accident.

4. The police did not give first aid at the scene.

5. The accident happened at 1500 hours.

ANSWERS:

1. ~~B~~ C

2. C

3. B

4. ~~B~~ A

5. A

## Analysing information question 6

You have 5 minutes to complete the question.

> A man of between 30 and 35 years of age was seen stealing a car from outside Mrs Brown's house yesterday. He was seen breaking the nearside rear window with a hammer before driving off at 40 miles per hour. He narrowly missed a young mother who was pushing a pram.

A = TRUE B = FALSE C = IMPOSSIBLE TO SAY

1. The man who stole the car was 34 years old.

2. He stole Mrs Brown's car.

3. The young mother who was pushing a pram was injured.

4. He used a hammer to smash the windscreen.

5. When he drove off he was breaking the speed limit.

ANSWERS:

1. C

2. C

3. B

4. B

5. C

**Analysing information question 7**

You have 5 minutes to complete the question.

> **A shopkeeper called Mr Smith was seen serving alcohol to a girl aged 16.**
>
> **The girl had shown him a fake ID, which was a driving licence belonging to her sister. The incident occurred at around 11.30pm on a Wednesday evening during December.**

A = TRUE B = FALSE C = IMPOSSIBLE TO SAY

1. The girl is old enough to purchase alcohol from Mr Smith.

2. The girl purchased the alcohol for her sister.

3. The girl's sister had given the driving licence to her.

4. Mr Smith will receive a custodial sentence for his actions.

ANSWERS:

1. B

2. C

3. C

4. C

## Analysing information question 8

You have 5 minutes to complete the question.

Following a bank robbery in a town centre, 6 masked gunmen were seen speeding away from the scene in a black van. The incident, which happened in broad daylight in front of hundreds of shoppers, was picked up by CCTV footage. Police are appealing for witnesses. The local newspaper has offered a £5,000 reward for any information leading to the conviction of all the people involved.

A = TRUE B = FALSE C = IMPOSSIBLE TO SAY

1. The car in which the gunmen drove off was a black van.

2. Someone must have seen something.

3. The incident was picked up by CCTV cameras.

4. The newspaper will pay £5,000 for information leading to the arrest of all of the men involved.

5. Police are not appealing to members of the public for help.

ANSWERS:

1. A

2. A ⊗ C

3. A

4. B

5. B

## Analysing information question 9

You have 5 minutes to complete the question.

A factory fire at 'Stevenage Supplies' was arson, the police have confirmed. A man was seen running away from the scene shortly before the fire started. Earlier that day a man was sacked from the company for allegedly stealing money from the safe. The incident is the second one to occur at the factory in as many months.

A = TRUE B = FALSE C = IMPOSSIBLE TO SAY

1. Police have confirmed that the fire at the factory was arson.

2. The man who was seen running away from the fire was the man who started it.

3. One previous 'fire-related' incident has already occurred at the factory.

4. The man who was sacked from the factory may have started the fire.

**ANSWERS:**

1. A

2. C

3. ~~B~~ e A

4. ~~B~~ C

## Analysing information question 10

You have 5 minutes to complete the question.

At 1800 hours today police issued a statement in relation to the crime scene in Armstrong Road. Police have been examining the scene all day and reports suggest that it may be murder. Forensic officers have been visiting the incident and informed us that the whole street has been cordoned off and nobody will be allowed through. Police say that the street involved will be closed for another 18 hours and no access will be available to anyone during this time.

A = TRUE B = FALSE C = IMPOSSIBLE TO SAY

1. Police have confirmed the incident as murder.

2. Forensic officers have now left the scene.

3. The road will be open at 12 noon the following day.

4. Although the street has been cordoned off, taxis and buses will be given access.

5. Forensic officers will be at the scene all night.

ANSWERS:

1.

2.

3.

4.

5.

## Analysing information question 11

You have 5 minutes to complete the question.

Mrs Rogers telephoned the police at 8pm to report a burglary at her house in Gamble Crescent. She reports that she came home from work and her front bedroom window was open but she doesn't remember leaving it open.

She informs the police that her jewellery box is missing and also £40 cash, which was left on the kitchen table. She left for work at 7am in the morning and arrived home at 5pm. No other signs of forced entry were visible.

A = TRUE  B = FALSE  C = IMPOSSIBLE TO SAY

1. The burglar made his/her way in through the bedroom window.

2. The burglar took the jewellery and £40 cash before leaving.

3. Mrs Rogers was away from the house for 10 hours in total.

4. Mrs Rogers may have left the window open herself before leaving for work.

5. There were other visible signs of forced entry.

ANSWERS:

1.

2.

3.

4.

5.

## Analysing information question 12

You have 5 minutes to complete the question.

**The local bank was held up at gunpoint on Monday the 18th of September at approximately 4pm. The thieves used a black motorcycle to make their getaway.**

**The following facts are also known about the incident:**

**- Two shots were fired.**

**- There were 12 staff members on duty at the time of the raid.**

**- The alarm was raised by the manager and the police were called.**

**- The cashier was ordered to hand over a bag of money containing £7,000.**

**- The thieves have not yet been caught.**

**- Police are appealing for witnesses.**

A = TRUE B = FALSE C = IMPOSSIBLE TO SAY

1. The thieves have been caught.

2. The cashier raised the alarm.

3. The cashier was shot.

4. Two people were injured.

5. The bank was open for business at the time of the incident.

ANSWERS:

1.

2.

3.

4.

5.

## Analysing information question 13

You have 5 minutes to complete the question.

A father and son were found dead in their two-bedroom flat in Sparsbrook on Sunday evening. They had both been suffocated.

The following facts are also known:

- The victims were identified by the police as Mark Webster, 16 years old, and his father, Thomas Webster, 39 years old.

- Thomas was in debt to the sum of £37,000.

- Two men were seen leaving the house at 4pm on Sunday afternoon.

- Two men were seen acting suspiciously in the area on Saturday evening before driving off in a Brown Ford Escort car.

- Thomas had previously contacted the police to express his concerns about his safety following threats from his creditors.

- The house had not been broken into.

A = TRUE  B = FALSE  C = IMPOSSIBLE TO SAY

1. The people Thomas owed money to could have been responsible for the deaths.

2. The two men seen leaving the house were not responsible for the deaths of Mark Webster and Thomas Webster.

3. The house had been broken into.

4. Neighbours reported two men acting suspiciously in the area on Saturday evening.

5. The people responsible for the deaths drove off in a brown Ford Escort car.

ANSWERS:

1.

2.

3.

4.

5.

## ANSWERS TO ANALYSING INFORMATION QUESTIONS

### Question 5

1. Impossible to say

2. Impossible to say

3. False

4. True

5. True

### Question 6

1. Impossible to say

2. Impossible to say

3. False

4. False

5. Impossible to say

### Question 7

1. False

2. Impossible to say

3. Impossible to say

4. Impossible to say

### Question 8

1. True

2. Impossible to say

3. True

4. False

5. False

### Question 9

1. True

2. Impossible to say

3. Impossible to say

4. True

## Question 10

1. False

2. Impossible to say

3. True

4. False

5. Impossible to say

## Question 11

1. Impossible to say

2. Impossible to say

3. True

4. True

5. False

## Question 12

1. False

2. False

3. Impossible to say

4. Impossible to say

5. Impossible to say

## Question 13

1. True

2. Impossible to say

3. False

4. Impossible to say

5. Impossible to say

## A FEW FINAL WORDS

You have now reached the end of the testing guide and no doubt you will be ready to take the language test element of the Scottish Police Test.

The majority of candidates who pass the police officer selection process have a number of common attributes. These are as follows:

### 1. They believe in themselves.

The first factor is self-belief. Regardless of what anyone tells you, you CAN become a police officer. Just like any job of this nature, you have to be prepared to work hard in order to be successful. Make sure you have the self-belief to pass the selection process and fill your mind with positive thoughts.

### 2. They prepare fully.

The second factor is preparation. Those people who achieve in life prepare fully for every eventuality and that is what you must do when you apply to become a police officer. Work very hard and especially concentrate on your weak areas.

### 3. They persevere.

Perseverance is a fantastic word. Everybody comes across obstacles or setbacks in their life, but it is what you do about those setbacks that is important. If you fail at something, then ask yourself 'why' you have failed. This will allow you to improve for next time and if you keep improving and trying, success will eventually follow. Apply this same method of thinking when you apply to become a police officer.

### 4. They are self-motivated.

How much do you want this job? Do you want it, or do you *really* want it?

When you apply to join the police you should want it more than anything in the world. Your levels of self-motivation will shine through on your application and during your interview. For the weeks and months leading up to the police officer selection process, be motivated as best you can and always keep your fitness levels up as this will serve to increase your levels of motivation.

Work hard, stay focused and be what you want...

The How2become Team

P.S. Don't forget, you can get FREE access to more tests online at: www.PsychometricTestsOnline.co.uk

# how2become

**Attend a 1 Day Police Officer Training Course at:**

**www.PoliceCourse.co.uk**

# NEED A LITTLE EXTRA HELP?
# PASS YOUR SCOTTISH
# POLICE ASSESSMENTS

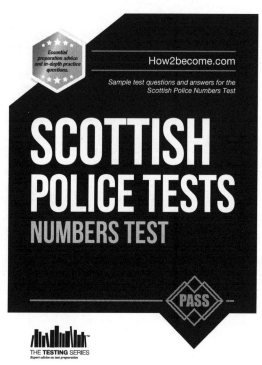

# FOR MORE INFORMATION ON OUR SCOTTISH
# POLICE GUIDES, PLEASE VISIT

# WWW.HOW2BECOME.COM

# Get Access To
# FREE
# Psychometric Tests

**www.PsychometricTestsOnline.co.uk**